Profits are Generosity, Entrepreneurship is Philanthropy: *The Principles of a World of Minimal Force and Maximum Voluntarism*

In Short… Be Nice, Don't Hurt, Don't Steal, Embrace Change

By Alex Merced

Introduction

I've never been one for long winded verbose proclamations of my principles, virtues and overall framework for looking at the world. In these writings I hope to present a straight to the point breakdown of my belief that a world centered around voluntary arrangements vs coerced arrangements is an ideal worth holding and pursuing. In this world when individuals seeking to better their lot in life through entrepreneurship succeed the result is giving society more than it had before. The profits of their efforts a symbol of the philanthropy that is entrepreneurship.

My influences in life are wide in variety, I often have trouble tracing back which ideas I got where. Some may have come from watching John Stossel as a child on 20/20, maybe from reading Ayn Rand's, "Anthem", when I was in high school. Ron Paul, F.A. Hayek, Ludwig Von

Mises, Mary Ruwart, Murray Rothbard, Milton Friedman, Douglass North, James Buchanan, Tom Woods, Robert Murphy, George Selgin, Deidre McCloskey, Russ Roberts, and Robert Nozick are among the many names that have influenced me over the years.

My time studying applied sociological/anthropological concepts in the popular culture studies department at Bowling Green State University certainly gave me tools to see the benefits to these ideas from different angles and to understand criticisms of them better.

My several efforts at entrepreneurship as an event planner, retail hobby store owner and broadcaster have all given me deeper conviction in open markets and their benefits to society and individuals.

This is the synthesis of the way I see the world and what it can be. This view has been shaped by my experiences and the ideas of those who came before me.

The Principles

If you lived on a stranded island on your own, things like property rights would not matter as there are no other individuals to dispute ownership with. Point being is that the principles I hope to discuss serve a purpose and that is to help society exist, establishing some rules for us all to live by so we can coexist and manage disputes and conflicts as peacefully as possible. While I will discuss conclusions that come out of these principles later on, and virtues that I encourage people to undertake, it's these basic principles that ideally underpin our every interaction with each other.

Self-Ownership

The root of everything starts with the assumption that we own ourselves (life and body). This is a powerful and necessary assumption as without it the door opens to ownership by another, and I suspect none of us want to be under the dominion of another knowing the atrocities in history that occur when that is the case. At least in self-defense this seems like a sound central principle to organize society around.

Non-Aggression

If people own themselves then their life and body is for each individual to do with as they please. From this we can set a rule for when the use of implicit violence and force is appropriate. If you own yourself it is appropriate to use force to defend yourself, but since another is not yours then initiating force upon their life or body would not be appropriate.

These two principles allow everyone in society to have the greatest autonomy possible while having clear easy to understand lines to resolve disputes when they occur. Although from these two principles one can derive many other values societies would likely develop under these conditions.

The Secondary Values

So if we lived in a world where we universally believe and operate under the idea that we own ourselves and should not initiate force on each other several things naturally follow.

Property Rights

So while it's clear that my life and body are mine how about all other scarce resources. Without some sort of clear system to determine what is mine and what is yours we're more likely to resort to violent disputes over anything around us as there is no other framework to do so. If I own myself and my body then I in turn own my effort known as labor. If I find some unclaimed resources and exert labor to lay the initial claim such as building a fence around unclaimed land then that becomes my property. This makes sense as there is no one else who can say they have a claim senior to mine. The claim I have on this property is an extension of my self-ownership resulting in no one else having the legitimate claim to initiate force upon it like my life and body.

Free Exchange

So eventually much of the unclaimed resources become claimed does this mean later generations are left to go without the ability to accumulate property? Not at all, an individual can take their property and voluntarily exchange or gift it to another. As long as people are free to exchange their property as they wish those with less property have the opportunity to accumulate whether by exchanging their labor or other property they may have. Another benefit of being able to freely exchange the vast array of property is that when a voluntary exchange occurs both parties enter the transaction with the expectation of being better off than without the transaction. The consent of both parties is a signal this will more likely be the case than not. If one were able to initiate or threaten force on another to attain or exchange property the likeliness the aggressed party is better off is likely slim.

Decentralization

If people can freely exchange property with whoever they wish this has the natural effect of decentralizing the provision of goods and services. As individuals and groups start enterprises to exchange with others there is nothing to prevent someone from seeking out multiple providers that may be cheaper, better quality, more convenient to deal with etc. Outside of the economic benefits of competition in the realm of free exchange it also provides society an important benefit in redundancy. Since free exchange will result in a decentralized network of providers, if any single provider ceases to exist it does not abruptly disrupt the operation of society.

Individualism

If we are self-owning individuals exchanging freely to achieve our goals, dreams and desires, there is need to take others as individuals as well. Since every person can be someone that we may be able to exchange with there is an incentive to maintain good relationships with as many individuals as possible which acts as a disincentive to dismiss people as members of collectives. While it may seem contradictory, the more we are uniquely responsible for ourselves the greater the need to maintain relationships with others and form community. Since any person has the power to make choices with their life and property that can positively or negatively affect me and vice versa.

Voluntarism

Everything mentioned before creates a world where the movement of society is based on the consent and voluntary choices of all its members. Voluntarism is not just good because of the decentralized networks of goods and services and stronger communities but also for the knowledge all of our choices create. Every success we achieve grants us knowledge so we can succeed more often, and with every failure the knowledge to fail less often. This is knowledge that would not be created if our outcomes were based on sheer compulsion of a central authority versus the voluntary choices each of us make.

The Voluntary Virtues

There are several virtues that I definitely encourage people to embrace. Every person can choose which virtues they find valuable but the ones I'll detail I feel contribute to not only enhancing a world built around the principles and values I previously outlined but also help maintain it.

Forgiveness

When people make choices they may have positive and negative outcomes. When someone makes mistakes or wrongs us we can quickly become angry or upsct at them and this can quickly become a call to limit one's choices or autonomy. The ability to forgive the imperfections of others allows us to preserve the principles of self-ownership.

Tolerance

People will not only will make mistakes but they may choose to live in ways that others may find undesirable, questionable and even offensive. When people exercise tolerance of the diversity self-ownership brings in every aspect of our lives it is more likely a world built around self-ownership can survive.

Empathy

The ability to see the actions of others through their eyes, to attempt to understand their motivations can go a long way in being able to tolerate and forgive.

Profits are Generosity, Entrepreneurship is Philanthropy

When two or more parties voluntarily exchange property, it is safe to assume that both parties entered the transaction expecting to be better off. If a party did not think they would be better off they would likely not engage in the transaction. If someone were to start an enterprise, it would make sense they would only be able to have repeat business if they are providing value for those they exchange with and vice versa. If the enterprise was worse off after the transaction they'd soon find themselves out of operation even if their exchange partners were pleased.

If an enterprise is able to sell their goods and services for a price that is greater than their expense to create said good or service that is profit. When there is a profit for the enterprise it means the enterprise can be sustained providing value for its patrons. What is more generous or philanthropic than creating a sustainable institution that provides value.

Many only see one sided transactions as generous, that one party must choose to be worse off for it to be called kindness or generous. While I Don't begrudge anyone who is willing to sacrifice for others I don't find its virtue any greater than a mutually beneficial transaction. When an organization is setup to provide value for others but funded by a third party, often referred to as a "charity" this presents a unique challenge.

When one donates to charity there is no certainty that the value provided is greater than the value given up. This is because often times the donor is giving for the "sense of value provided" than actual value provided to them which is subjectively valuable but impossible to measure vs value provided to the recipients of the charity. Also, there is the issue of sustainability as those getting the charities services aren't the determinant of whether the charity continues but the willingness of donors to give and what they want from the charity doesn't always line up with the recipients. So while charities are great and I encourage their existence... the accountability, sustainability and measurability of an enterprise entering mutual exchange is greater thus results in a greater level of generosity in my opinion.

When I say profit is generosity and entrepreneurship is philanthropy, I sincerely mean it in its truest sense.

State, Government and Dystopia

So now we understand the Principles, Values and Virtues I think would make for a world of maximum value to all individuals. Many times people seek to outsource the use of force initially in self-defense. These institutions of outsourced violence often times stray from their initial purpose and use force to control and shape society. Before we delve deeper let's clarify a few terms as I'll be using them.

When people delegate an institution to be the sole institution with the authority to use force that will be referred to as "The State".

An institution that governs by establishing rules and standards in a particular area or people regardless of its means of doing so is a "government".

The reason it is important to separate these terms is to clarify that violence is not a necessary tool for governing and those authorized to use violence don't solely use it for governing.

Rules and Standards

There is nothing in itself wrong with rules and standards as they help us interact with each other in every aspect of our lives. The fact that there is a standard definition for most of the words in the English language makes it possible to communicate in the written manner and I'm not required to define every single word as I go along. If a board game did not have rules there would be no way to determine who is winning and losing which would eliminate a lot of the fun of the game.

Although, some rules and standards work better than others. Simple rules are easier to understand thus easier to follow and enforce while complex rules are hard to understand thus whether they are being followed correctly can be a constant question. Rules with little room for discretion leaves less room for favoritism by arbiters of the rules, while those which leave lots of room for discretion create room for favoritism and corruption.

Although like anything rules and standards improve when people are allowed to try different rules and see what works well and what doesn't. This is why decentralization is important as it allows discovery.

Non-Violent Enforcement

There are several ways rules and standards are established, enforced, and discovered in a decentralized non-violent way. When someone or some organization is behaving in a way that violates the societal values and norms of the time transparency, exclusion and alternatives can be used to hold them accountable.

By educating others about the discouraged actions of others, people can make different choices leading to changes in the target's actions or punitive consequences in the form of exclusion.

Exclusion means not patroning a business or organization or not allowing someone to patron a business or organization for violating the values and norms of the day. People who are isolated can either conform to norms but if they feel norms should be changed can create an alternative.

By creating alternative businesses and organizations that cater to different norms, it allows individuals through their choices to participate and decide whether norms should change or remain. These are only a handful of the possible ways to provide enforcement of rules formal and informal without the use of violence and how these methods spur discovery in themselves.

The State as Government

Governments surround us, the board of directors of every company and non-profit is a government of that organization providing rules and standards. Although often times when governing large geographic areas people establish a state to act as its government. By delegating each individual's right to defend their life, body and property to the state it starts as an institution to do exactly that. The problem comes in when those who created the state are long gone yet future generations are still subject to and some in control of the delegated violence of those long gone. Those individuals within the state become more and more distant from the original intention of the state making its use of violence slowly but surely stray away from violence as a tool of defense to violence as a tool of centralization and control.

Taxation

While the state is delegated the use of violence, its ability to use it requires armaments and personnel that require resources to be attained. While an enterprise can raise funds to be used by its governing bodies through investment and then in payment for the goods and services it provides, a state generally doesn't initially provide good or services beyond mutual defense so to raise the necessary resources exercises a credible threat of violence to extort them... it engages in taxation. The state will begin arbitrarily making claims of resources on different economic exchanges such as sales, income and trade and threaten force if those claims aren't made. This can be seen as the original sin of the state, the first time a state uses violence for non-defense purposes that creates the precedent and appetite to expand its use.

The Regulatory State

While in the early days government begins as a tool of defending one from another but eventually that cry for defense stretches beyond preventing direct force on the life, body and property of another. Challenges and tragedies eventually occur in the day to day of people's lives and this results in an outcry for rules and standards which is a fine response. Although, instead of the allowing a decentralized process discover which rules should exist and what institutions should enforce them people rush to demanding the state to create the rules and enforce them with the threat of violence.

This happens because of the expediency of violence. People fear that they won't immediately follow the rules unless the threat of violence is behind it resulting in bypassing the process that would have held those rules accountable. People eventually discover that these rules impose costs on those subject to them creating an economic advantage for those who aren't subject to them or have more resources to absorb the costs. This will turn into everyone calling everything a crisis to create rules to impose costs on actors they don't like or on early stage competition before it becomes a threat.

Having s regulatory state cuts short the process of rule discovery and accountability while also becoming a tool for people to levy additional costs on those they don't like.

The Warfare State

While a State builds up its personnel and armaments it becomes easier and easier to make the decision to go into full scale violent conflict better known as war. Like anything, the more capable you are of taking an action the more likely you'll take that option. Once a war begins large enterprises will expand around providing the tools of war and will become dependent on the existence of future conflicts to maintain their growth. This is what is often referred to as the military-industrial complex, the political weight that accrues when the military sector becomes such a large employer and economic force that those with influence or control of the state have a hard time escaping its influence.

This is the nature of a state when it gets involved in anything. Due to its ability to extract resources through the use of violence it allows it to infuse any sector of the economy with large amounts of resources that result in a dependency of that expenditures continuance. This dependency results in the creation of political organizing to ensure that if these expenditures are ever threatened alarmist cries will beat agents of the state from ever going back. Once a state gets involved it is hard for it to ever rollback its involvement.

The Welfare State

When people feel that existing charitable efforts aren't alleviating the plight of a group of people quickly or effectively enough inevitably cries for larger scale welfare programs begin. Programs of this scale require an organization with large amounts of resources so the state becomes the easy target as to who should provide the resources and operate the program. The problem is enterprises begin to be engineered to be on the receiving end of these programs becoming dependent on their existence. On top of this without competition these programs lack the decentralized discovery process that allows for efficiency and innovation making these programs often times more expensive relative to the aid provided.

The Cost of Living

The costs of things we need such as food, shelter, education and healthcare affect the quality of life and the different faces of the state can affect the cost of living. The regulatory state imposes costs on enterprises that often result in higher costs to their consumers. The growing taxation needed to fund the welfare and warfare state reduce people's incomes to pay the rising costs and as well as increases costs as enterprises attempt to recoup the taxes they pay. As People's incomes get crowded out by the cost of living and taxation, they will become less charitable making the demand for more welfare inevitable and the taxes that come with it. As people struggle for income, they become more willing to engage in less ethical behaviors in the form of crime. The increase in crime results in creating more demand for regulations and the tax and cost increases that come with it. The state in its many faces results in perpetuating the many problems people want it to solve creating a downward spiral that is hard to turn around.

Other eventual problems with states

States will naturally form when a group of individual decides to delegate their use of defensive violence, bound on future generations will often evolve into using this power beyond defense and develop into warfare, regulatory and welfare states. The cost of the growing state is often funded with confiscated wealth via taxation leading to lower incomes paying a growing cost of living.

States create even more problems beyond this fatal flaw. The more areas of society that the state gets involved in, the poorer its governance becomes because the best use of resources for something like Warfare can conflict with the best use of those resources for something like welfare or regulation creating internal conflicts affecting the quality of decisions made in each area. This is like the saying, "those who do too much do little well".

But it goes beyond just being stretched too thin as an organization but also the level of power a state can exercise in any area of society attracts primarily those who will personally benefit from influencing this power over others, making the state almost inevitably corrupt over time.

At the end of the day states will form and as they become bigger, more intrusive and more expensive they will inevitably collapse on themselves when taxation creep can no longer keep pace with expenditure creep. Just by the mere fact of being aware of these trends you can take action to insulate your own life of its impact.

Human Action and Motivation

Now I want discuss the framework of human action, of looking at the world as the result of endless individual actions based on subjective values shaping individual motivation. This way of breaking down the world and its phenomena was pioneered by a tradition of economic thought known as the "Austrian School" which includes great economists like Carl Munger, Ludwig Von Mises and F.A. Hayek.

Why Human Action Matters

At the end of the day all human economic and social phenomena can be traced back to the individual choices that we all make. When we say something, buy something or do something it is with purpose. My every action is me applying means to an end and this gives us the insight to breakdown historic, economic and social trends.

Subjective Value

One of the most valuable insights of economist Carl Menger is the realization that nothing has a universal value to the individual. How good, valuable and virtuous any good, service or action is exists purely in my perception and can't be directly compared the quantity of value another perceives for the same item. So how much I personally value apples may be different than how you value apples.

Displayed Preference

While we can't determine an absolute value of any action, we can certainly determine the relative value. When presented with a choice of an Apple or an Orange, we can determine if I choose the Orange that I at least value the Orange relatively more than the Apple in this context. These displayed preferences allow us to extrapolate small bits of knowledge from every choice people make. If I had been forced to eat the apple or not given the option there would be no way of knowing this relative valuation. Even if you asked me, what I say may be different than the action I may take. Bottom line, free people making choices creates knowledge which can be used to make future choices.

Exchange

If value is subjective than the result of voluntary exchanges in goods and services is that both parties walk away with what they perceive as more valuable. If this is the case a world of free Exchange allows the world's resources to reshuffle to those who value them the most.

Money and Prices

Medium of Exchange

When entering exchanges with others it can be cumbersome trying to find the precise good or service to exchange for the things one demands. Overtime there is a good that becomes universally valued and becomes something that when received in exchange can be used to exchange for something else you may want later. This good is facilitating much more efficient and quick exchange, allowing for goods to travel to those who value them quicker.

Store of Value

Sometimes the good you have to exchange is perishable giving you a limited time to exchange it before it loses its value (think fruits). The longer the good lasts the more of its value your able to use in exchange for a longer period of time. Goods which do not deteriorate allow you to wait as long as you want to exchange it, this is called being a store of value. This allows people to take the value of their labor and set it aside for later times instead of rushing to exchange it before it wastes.

Unit of Account

Often when exchanging, the value of what you are receiving varies so when you find a good store of value it helps if it's easily to divisible into measurable amounts to accommodate. Eventually standard divisions develop and it becomes the way to express the value of different goods, values, debts, etc. It becomes a unit of account.

Money

A good or service that acts as a medium of exchange, store of value and unit of account is often referred to as, "money". What drives the demand and use of a money is its ability to serve these three functions.

Prices

When people use standard units of money to express the prevailing value of goods and services these are known as "prices".

Prices as Vehicles of Knowledge

Prices change as circumstances change. People are limited in their knowledge and experience and aren't always aware of changing circumstances and don't have the natural foresight to adjust behavior without that awareness. Prices fix this problem.

Imagine a farm that is the sole producer of a particular fruit has a drought. There will not be enough of the fruit for all buyers at their typical levels of consumption. The farmer to survive will have to charge more for his remaining crops to make up for those loss. This results in the grocery having to charge more for the fruit, which will lead to many consumers naturally choosing to cut back their consumption to save money. In this situation everyone reduced how many fruits they bought leading more people to be able to buy fruits without the consumer needing to understand the drought. The knowledge and the appropriate response were transmitted via the price.

If the price had not changed at all everyone would have attempted normal consumption of the limited supply of fruits. The first few buyers would have had their normally desired quantity without leaving any left for the remaining consumers.

Contrary, If the farmer had a high crop yield then he would naturally lower the price to make sure every unit was sold. The lower price would make consumers consider consuming more since it costs less to do so leading to all the fruits being consumed instead of wasted.

If the price is not raised the normal consumer would have bought their normal amount leaving many fruits unsold to be wasted.

Prices, when allowed to move freely based on real world realities help coordinate individual choices in line with scarce resources which is why prices should be allowed to roam freely within free exchange.

Time and Interest

Some may be able to accumulate so much wealth that they can't or don't want to consume all of it and others may have a need of resources for a variety of different reasons. In this situation those who need resources can borrow them from those who have excess. The cost of borrowing these resources for a period of time is called, "interest".

One way to think of interest is the price in future money that one must pay for the use of today money. There are several factors that would affect the rate of interest that prevails in the market.

Time Preference

Some may want to consume the wealth they've accumulated. If there is something you really want to buy now, you are exhibiting a high time preference and it may require more interest to convince you to lend your wealth over consuming it. While if you have nothing you particularly want to buy now then you may decide to lend it more easily at lower rates due to your lower time preference. The prevailing interest rate signals the general time preference of market participants.

Liquidity Preference

People often times may want to keep some money available for rainy days so they will not consume or invest these funds (although if held at a financial institution then that institution will lend the funds instead). If individuals and institutions fear economic uncertainty, they may decide to hold money instead of making it available for lending.

Opportunity Cost of Other Investments

If equity-based investments (stocks) are performing really well due to a strong economy then those seeking to borrow funds may have to pay more interest to persuade a potential lender to choose making a loan over buying stock.

Risks

While the factors previously mentioned will affect the general or natural rate of interest, the rate of interest for any particular loan will then add on a "risk premium" for the relative risks of the particulars loan.

Intervention

If a money supply is discretionary (meaning there is a particular entity that can control it), it is possible for those with monetary discretion to manipulate interest rates. By increasing the money in circulation, they can lower the rate of interest and Vice Versa.

Mal-investment

Interest rates are prices like anything else and coordinate human action by transmitting knowledge of time preference, liquidity preference, economic performance, and risk which affect how people will make use of loanable funds. In the same way prices not allowed to naturally move would cause fruit shortages or surpluses for the farmer, intervention in the rate of interest can cause a different selection of borrowers and projects for the lender that may not be in line with realities on the ground. This miscoordination will result in mal-investment which in the short term may appear as an increase in economic activity but will not be sustainable as the miscoordination of resources reveals itself over time.

Without the knowledge of the free market prices that would have existed absent intervention it is near impossible to identify what would be the sustainable investments even if one anticipated the mal-investment and the consequences to come.

In Conclusion

Money allows society to have prices which transmit knowledge and help society coordinate in a decentralized manner. Interest rates are a price signal like any other and has consequences when manipulated.

The End

I hope you enjoyed this brief overview of the way I see the world around me shaped by many of the Philosophers and Economists I named earlier on in this publication who I recommend you read to go deeper in depth on many of the ideas discussed here. Following I'll include a collection useful quotes from my social media posts over the years that relate to many of the ideas I've discussed in this book. At the end of the day one of the best things you can do to make the world a better place is by being the best you possible and inspiring others to be better. You can also participate in your community and help organize people to overcome challenges together before other institutions force their involvement. Fix the world before the wrong people try to fix it.

QUOTES FROM ALEX MERCED

"In a world of free association, you have choices but they do have consequences. Participation in certain institutions may come with requirements that not meeting results in the inability participate. You are free to choose to opt out of those requirements and not participate but you are not entitled to opt out and still require that institution to let you participate.

This is actually how many controversial requirements are already upheld, without compulsion but with the possibility of non-association. Schools, Universities, etc. can place their requirements and you can choose to participate or not. If the requirements are too high the institution will find continued existence difficult and that's the give and take of a free society."

"I feel that modern economics has evolved beyond just production. when you look at like the institutional school and lot of the literature on corporate governance and public choice, it appears to me it's always less about the macro production picture (which it is to many) and more about the context that individual decisions get made about scarce resources and how that context affects those decisions.

So yeah, I hate terms like capitalism and socialism because there is much more nuance to individual action and what influences it that comparing any two countries with different institutional, cultural and geographical differences make individual actions behave completely different than the next.

To further elaborate, economic decision making will look different from place to place and from person to person. The particular arrangements matter less to me than the ability to change and adapt to a changing context.

Governance and Economic decision making that is as close to the individual possible to me just makes sense as the way any society would be most nimble to rearrange and change as needed while larger more centralized decision making may theoretically have some scale benefits but is often slower to adapt and quicker to oppress to resist adaptation.

So yeah, I just want free people to do what free people do. Free exchange, pricing, and a system of property just seem to be the logical conclusion of that but if circumstances change and free people chose something else, I wouldn't be overly bothered."

"I'm more than glad to respect people on their own terms because that often breeds reciprocity for them to respect me on mine even when we don't see eye to eye on everything and I may not always fully understand their preferences. While there are certainly cultural debates to be had and societal shifts that'll be determined by our individual preferences and decisions in aggregate.

Most of what I see labeled as a "culture war" is all sides trying to justify why they don't even halfway try to understand the perspective, experiences and concerns of those who challenge their views of what norms should and must be. All sides are visibly at fault with their rush to call names, exaggerated claims of what those they disagree with are saying, and their unwillingness to even fathom a world where we all coexist peacefully.

Pox on all houses, huts and shacks."

"Here is the problem with longtime feuds between groups. They may be silly and counterproductive but they eventually die down as people involved in them learn to ignore each other and coexist in a level of shared space (peace doesn't always have to mean liking each other).

New entrants into both groups often learn about the feud, feel they can magically repair or fix the rift and usually reopen the wounds, scorn and resentment allowing for another generation of division.

I see this with political movement communities, I see this between nations, etc.

This is why Individualism is important to me. Once any aspect of our identity doesn't own us so much as to drive the need to perpetuate divisions and active conflict to feel that you are living up to how you see yourself we'll all be in a better place.

Why, because we realize that we have nothing to prove to ourselves, we can just accept ourselves as we are individually and realize our labels are part of us not all of us.

(Often the best thing you can do to fix a feud is ignore it and not participate so it fades away with those who cling to it)"

"Pro-Tip: If you don't like someone other people like you don't need to obsessively trash them. Instead spend the time talking about whoever or whatever you do like.

Trashing others...

- Makes you look like a jerk
- Gives the target more publicity, which you probably don't want

The best thing to do with people you don't like is to keep them irrelevant by ignoring them."

"People always ask me whether I lean right or lean left, and I don't think I lean either way. When it comes to many underlying social critiques and concerns on both sides there is stuff that I think of as fair and valid and stuff that I feel jumps the shark.

Regarding valid concerns I often don't see them as mutually exclusive. I think we should aim for a more tolerant, compassionate, and empathetic culture and aim to create that with my example but I also think that it's important to foster an openness to discussing controversial and uncomfortable topics and opinions. Without that openness to speak to one another, ideas won't change because no one is willing to engage and tolerate others enough to act as a model of openness and tolerance.

I'm never a big fan of isolation and shaming as a mode of cultural change. This may be better than violence and control, but that doesn't make it ideal. I don't want anyone feeling so isolated and shameful that they can't say what's on their mind. If so, we can't identify where reflection or a good example can save someone from themselves and benefit others from being able to retain their peaceful involvement in society.

It's similar to my thoughts on prohibition. The ill effects of prohibition don't only occur if a good/service is outrightly prohibited but also if the costs become artificially high. Prohibiting speech explicitly or implicitly with isolation/shame (creating a high cost to speech) can also create speech black markets that only reinforce themselves making outcomes worse and the problem less transparent.

I want open markets, I want open speech, I want an open society because openness allows transparency and accountability for solutions to arise.

(Of course I don't want anyone to hurt anyone else, but we can much better prevent the violence of others if we can more easily see the warning signs and work them through which may occur when we engage openly in good faith.)"

"Order isn't created out of strict enforcement of every rule, it's about the buy-in of those subject to the rules that is dictated by the reasonableness of the rules and enforcement.

People lose faith in an institution, it dies. Faith dies when:

- When reasonable rules are not enforced

- When unreasonable rules are enforced

- When subjects feel they cannot change what they don't like about the institution

- When those with the most power are seen using that power advantage themselves at the expense of subjects

This applies to governments, enterprise and non-profit organizations. Remember this when someone wants to discuss the rule of law."

"Too many people get wrapped in the wrong question when it comes to the discussion of borders. That question is "does the Nation State have the right or duty to enforce and protect its borders". While it's fun to discuss whether Nation States have legitimate claims to government land, it really comes down to a difference of whether you believe the autonomy and property of future generations can be bound by agreements and pacts over the autonomy and property of prior generations. Most people aren't going to be on the absolute end of either side resulting in such a diverse discussion that it serves no purpose in resolving the policy question that is on the table.

"To the extent that Nation States exist whether you like them or not, what should border policy be?"

So my personal sentiment is that a more permissive policy with minimal barriers is better economically and in the long run creates a grander peace as cultures learn to coexist over generations (it's not quick and it's not pretty but does happen). Although this is the result of my more classically liberal and pluralistic values. It is totally rational and reasonable for someone to value the short run certainty cultural uniformity and limited labor competition can provide them at the expense of the grander but more distributed benefits of liberalism. (Basically, some may prefer more for them at the expense of more for everyone).

So to the extent whether I or someone else believes a Nation State should exist, they do. They will employ some sort of border policy but should it be generous and welcoming or punishing, strict and limited. Depends on your values, but let's have an actual conversation instead of shutting down conversation with words like Fascist, Communist, Racist, etc.

I will try to convince you to think my way and you are free to do your best to get me to think your way."

"While I love talking dollars and cents of policy many stats can't be determined in any absolute way (data collection is too imperfect) but it shouldn't matter when it comes to an individual's rights.

People's right to pursue opportunity, attain property, and improve their lot in life should not hinge on a math equation.

If math determined the right to free speech was a net cost, I would still fight for that right.

If math determined micromanaging life was absolutely a nct bcncfit I would still fight against it.

I just can't get behind the idea of squashing the dreams and motivations of individuals as a result of falling on the wrong side of arbitrary lines and rules that don't allow room for individual context to be considered."

"Metaphors matter in how we see, approach and solve life's challenges. Imagine that your challenges in life are like being stuck inside a room.

If you see four walls, no doors and no way out you'll feel hopeless and depressed

If you see doors but they are all locked with keys only others have you'll feel frustrated, stuck and lacking control

If you see doors that aren't easy to open but can be with just enough effort you'll feel hopeful and determined.

If you see many doors that you can just walk through... well, good for you!"

"Cultural appropriation alarmism is based on the idea we can't fully appreciate the experience of another so we shouldn't perform, celebrate or consume it. Problem is, the only experience we can truly appreciate is our own individual experience, why should that preclude me from taking/giving what I can from/to everyone else?

At the end of the day the heart of this is truly economic protectionism, limiting the competition to satisfy consumers. This time instead of consumers of goods or services, consumers of culture. Like when guilds/unions would decry non-guild members performing the service they perform. Like all protectionism it is sold as everything but.

Be courteous, respectful and decent. Also, feel free to celebrate and embrace each other's differences and mix and match them into something new, unique and beautiful."

"I see people becoming overly PC and the result is the feeling of judgement is making people more frustrated and less willing to try because they feel "it will never be enough."

I see people going out of their way to be anti-PC and I see people frustrated with trying to build bridges because "if they aren't going to try, why should I?"

I'm trying, I'm trying to show you ALL respect and tolerance whether you show it to me or not because someone has to start the process. We can't always wait for someone else to try or for them to immediately reciprocate when you do.

Civility, kindness and all the other qualities that shape the world towards a greater trend of peace and liberalism require effort and patience.

Start now, we'll get there faster."

"Populist is a word people use to describe many of the candidates running for office in recent times. While it's clear the message of a Donald Trump or Bernie Sanders can be quite different, they are both clearly populist messengers.

A populist message is signaled by two characteristics:

- A scapegoat for all the problems people feel.

- The answer being politically punishing the scapegoat as a magical bullet solution.

Here is the prototype of different populist messages...

Right-wing populism: The reason your life is so hard is that poor minorities and immigrants are taking advantage of your tax dollars while trade deals with other nations result in jobs leaving. The answer is to keep the immigrants out, end welfare and strong-arm trade with other nations in our favor. Vote for me, you don't need to do anything.

Left-wing populism: The reason your life is hard is that rich white corporate executives have lobbied for trade deals that let them exploit cheap labor overseas taking your jobs cutting your welfare to cut taxes for those corporations, fund wars for those corporations and deport immigrants back to lower wage countries for further exploitation by those corporations. We need to tax these corporations to restore your welfare and regulate them so they have to give you a high paying job. Vote for me, you don't need to do anything.

Libertarian Populism: The Government is inherently corrupted by all sorts of special interests has been interests to serve those interests resulting in taxes, regulations and other policies that make it too expensive to start businesses, employ labor, and pursue all levels of opportunity. We need to reduce the size and scope of government so those opportunities can be available again. Vote for me, you don't need to do anything.

The problem with a purely populist message, even a libertarian one is that it puts all the necessary change solely on government policy. This takes away any sense of personal responsibility for one's life outcomes leaving them to believe there is nothing they should be doing to improve their lives beyond voting for their favorite populist.

This is why populism sells, because it's appealing to believe that the only thing you need to do to change your life is Vote. While voting can have a very real impact on the world around us, at the end of the day our own lives are still very much within our own control despite very real challenges created by policy. Also, any change in any direction cannot sustainably work without each of us taking responsibility over what is within our control.

Populism sells, but populism sucks"

"How you treat others breeds reciprocity. I aim to breed reciprocity of kindness, Tolerance and forgiveness. Create a better world by being a better person and example. This reciprocity breeds a world of unrivaled liberalism."

"Tolerance doesn't mean agreement, and it doesn't mean not voicing criticism. It's saying that disagreement isn't the test on whether we can interact and coexist."

"Sometimes being Libertarian and trying to help others see the power they can unleash in themselves can be frustrating. Despite that, it's the right message for the right reasons, so I'll always push forward."

"As long as politics is about fighting over the reins of power over each other it will be dominated by polarization and fear. When it becomes about making the case to each other to voluntarily collaborate we'll have achieved libertarianism filled with hope."

"Remember compound returns. The gains now may seem small and meaning less but it builds upon itself and eventually becomes large and meaningful if you just keep growing. Never stop growing no matter how steep the hill may seem."

"Leadership isn't telling people to do things better, it isn't highlighting the failure of others and proclaiming yourself wiser. Leadership is not waiting for others and executing your vision and letting your example inspire others."

"I just want people to be free to exchange, to organize, to love and to do anything else they damn well please with their life, body and property."

"The status quo sells you fear in hopes you'll give up the reigns over your life. Libertarians preach there is hope in your hands and in your actions, aiming to inspire you to take those reigns back. Take back your power and empower others."

"Taxes reduce your income. The cost of living increases from regulations, licensing and government loan programs also reduce your income. This means the need to work longer hours keeping you from your passions, family and community. Vote Libertarian."

"A Libertarian wants you to make more choices in your life not because you'll always make the right ones, but because when you don't you will learn and make better choices. If everyone makes better choices, we all grow together."

"Being a strong team doesn't mean you always agree on the path forward. You discuss, you debate and you may even get angry. What makes a good team is everyone respects each enough to come back the next day to work towards a shared mission."

"I'm a Libertarian because I want to promote a HELLO Culture (Hope, Empowerment, Liberty, Love and Opportunity). Say GOODBYE to those other parties and join me in building that HELLO culture."

"Voting defensively to prevent worse only allows you to end up with "less bad". "Less bad" still gets worse and worse overtime. Only by voting offensively for better, good and best can we break from stagnation to growth, from volatility to stability, from fear to hope."

"I rather talk and exalt what is libertarian than bring attention to the things that aren't. Empowering yourself with enterprise, solving problems by voluntarily cooperating, enabling travel, trade, accumulating property and defending that property is libertarian."

"I'm not here to provoke, offend and disgust you with my opinions. I aim to endear, enamor and captivate you with the hope for the world of peace, voluntarism and opportunity that liberty brings in its wake."

"Change, Growth and Transformation begins with deciding to do things differently to be better and an example of how others can be better."

"How can the world change if the people in that world can't change it in their every action. Libertarianism is the only path that truly presents change because it's the only path willing to give people the freedom to create the changes they want."

"True change requires a long-term effort to break down status quo inertia. Voting Libertarian does exactly that. Voting Libertarian elects libertarians, topples ballot access barriers and sends a signal on the desire for autonomy. Every vote counts towards disruption."

"Think really hard about how you wish others were. Their manners, their attitude, their character. Imagine that, and make that the example you set for others."

"You can tax more and when you can't, print more money but you can't print doctors, teachers or food. You can easily distort and destroy the incentives for people create more of these things. Prosperity emerges from freedom and reciprocity, not from design."

"No President, dictator or tyrant can make your individual rights void at the stroke of a pen. They can merely attempt to scare you from exercising them by paying people with guns money they took from you to scare you and possibly cage you. Don't let fear win."

"So when are you a Libertarian?

A question that is debated when people discuss the idea of "thin" versus "thick" libertarianism. Those in the thin camp argue that libertarianism is simply a rejection of the initiation of violence. (you don't think the world's problems are solved by having someone else hurt others and take their stuff to force your ideals). While those in the "thick" camp argue that libertarianism should go further into stronger advocacy for the oppressed, multiculturalism, essentially really advocating that people can and should make an effort not just coexist but thrive together.

I agree with both, I just feel they are answering very different questions.

The "thin" crowd is arguing for a strict and clear definition of being libertarian as a view on the use of violence in governing society (violence is bad). They don't want other virtues or social values to be added in because then it becomes unclear and drives people into a never-ending fight on definitions. This bothers the "thick" crowd because someone with social or cultural views they may abhor can fall within the libertarian banner as long as they don't think violence and especially violence through government is the answer to bringing upon their worldview. Although we can't redefine every aspect of ourselves to reduce commonalities with those we don't like. I'm a male, and there are other males who've raped, murdered, etc. but I don't suggest people redefine male to exclude those who do those things.

Although I do think the particular social virtues and values you promote play a role in building a world where Libertarianism can grow and thrive. One of the things that brings many to look into libertarianism is when they begin to see the effects that individual freedom has on general welfare. Many of these effects come from the network effects of markets, the exchange of good, services and ideas that create wealth and innovation. The smaller that network of interacting individuals the smaller these effects may become.

So to illustrate when I'm getting at I'll make use of a rhetorical tool called a "reductio" (taking things to their extreme). Let's imagine a world where everyone rejects violence but their personal values and virtues still lead to isolated communities that voluntarily don't trade, don't travel, don't talk. Many of the most positive effects of the market may not quite play out leading to less prosperous communities which can lead to an environment where the isolation and struggle leads to a reversal on the use of violence. (it's easier to use violence on people you don't know and especially when your struggling)

Throw in tolerance, forgiveness, empathy and pluralism in the virtues we promote, it may be beyond the scope of libertarianism but would contribute to an environment where libertarianism can sustainably be a value that travels generation to generation. The market network effects will create prosperity and non-violence that would reinforce continuing down that path. The interaction of individuals makes calls for violence that much more difficult.

Will the world hit either extreme, probably not. Although in the hopes of a sustainable libertarianism it seems valuable to want to push in the direction of the later extreme."

"Being Libertarian is being ok with people making mistakes and being humble enough to realize you may not always know what is a mistake."

"Markets are empowering, when you have access to them. The Inequities and what feels like economic injustice is not because of markets, it's because so many didn't have access to them for so long. Limited market access is what created inequality, open up access."

"When an addict quits drugs, they go through great short term pain for worthwhile long term gains. Voting against two party corruption is the same, if you don't start the process in fear of short run pain you never get the long run benefits."

"Free Markets are not about corporate control, it's about consumer control. Consumers choose who they give power too, and if no good choices exist, they are able to become a producer and offer an alternative to their fellow consumers. This is how we grow together."

"Improving the world isn't about fault or punishment but reflecting on what actions we can take to contribute to the things we want and which actions contribute to what we don't want that we should stop. Focusing on blame/punishment distracts from solutions."

"To be a true lover of freedom one must develop a deep tolerance and even enthusiasm for what is possible in the certainty of uncertainty."

"The world evolves by the example we set. If we set an example of violence, hate and intolerance then that's what will spread. I want a world of peace, love and tolerance and that is the example I aim to set and win by."

"Not having the wealth, income, goods or services you'd like doesn't mean you aren't free. If barriers are placed in your way to work towards things you want like taxes, regulations and licensing making you stuck where you are, THEN you may be limited in your freedom."

"Many people talk about people having equal access to things like healthcare and education. I don't want equal, I want people to seek the best they can get. I do want open access to goods and services like health and education with as little barriers as possible."

"People have given up hope of their elected officials doing good, and instead vote on the promise of who will do less harm. As long as you allow the system to make that your choice, that's the choice it will present you."

"I aim to promote love. Although, Tolerance isn't love but the ability to coexist. People deeply undervalue the worth of coexistence in today's world. I promote love, but tolerance is a win/win for everyone."

"A better world will never be created by violence. Despite our differences we should always aim for civil discourse in hopes of helping each other to evolve based on ideas. I condemn those who today attempted to use violence to cut that discussion short."

"The most important tools you have for changing how people think and behave are metaphors and your example. Metaphors often internally control how we interpret the world around us, and people emulate those they respect, admire and even envy."

"I want a world where we exchange ideas, goods and services freely with each other. Where we relish in the relationships we develop with each other more and judge the relationship and lives of others less. Where knowledge accumulates rapidly from our choices. Freedom."

"The left recently complained about "whataboutism", the pointing out that left administrations did many of the same bad policies as the current right wing one. (Cronyist trade dealings, mass deportations, global intervention, massive deficits, accommodative monetary policy, etc.)

This is Important because why should I listen to someone telling me to vote differently if what they are telling to vote for will get me the same? I vote Libertarian in the hopes of actually electing someone that will do something different such as intervene less in the affairs of other nations, promote actual free trade, balance the budget and let interest rates be set by markets.

The odds may be high, but if things go my way, even a little, at least there will be genuine substantive change versus merely a change in tone, rhetoric and in whose cronies get political favors."

"To the extent anyone promotes non-violence, voluntarism and peace in our everyday interactions, they are my ally. To the extent they promote violence, war and theft they will find in me a loud antagonist. Why, because I'm a Libertarian."☐☐

"Regime change, prohibition, and closed trade are policies that have and continue to contribute to hostilities between nations and on borders. We ignore fixing these policies at our own peril."☐☐

"Most people believe people just behave the way they behave so they must be controlled and punished when out of line. Libertarians understand people respond to incentives and expectations. Market incentives and expecting self-responsibility makes us better."☐☐

"Tight immigration policies are like restricting or banning any good or service, it creates black markets. This article details how tighter border controls are leading to growing organized crime, extortion and violence around immigration. Illegal immigration is a black market, the ill-effects of black markets can only be fixed with the less restrictions, less prohibition and more freedom. When will we learn... prohibition doesn't work!"

"Libertarian political action is about moving the conversations regarding solutions of societies challenges away from compulsory means to voluntary means."

"Libertarians are not against public goods... they question whether centralized monopolistic government is the best institution to provide them and whether taxation is an ethical or effective way of funding it.

Libertarians are not against regulations... they question whether centralized monopolistic government is the best institution that can create fair rules that are fairly enforced and whether it's able to respond quickly when it gets things wrong.

Libertarians aren't against assisting those who aren't well off... but questions whether centralized monopolistic government can do so efficiently and effectively and whether the level of taxation needed to fund inefficiency is ethical and creates more poor people in the process.

A decentralized competitive market of voluntary institutions such as enterprise, charity and community can provide public goods, Regulations and Welfare. While each institution may provide only a small piece in aggregate, the quantity will be greater and quicker to respond when something works or doesn't.

Libertarians aren't just about what people should have but how it shouldn't be provided (without the inefficiency of involuntarism)."

"Libertarianism just tells us the absolute minimum we should explicitly expect from each other which is just the expectation of non-aggression. Libertarianism places no limits on the beauty or ugliness we can create within the bounds of voluntarism."

"Libertarianism isn't complicated, we just believe Consent truly matters as a principle not as political political rhetoric to attain power."

"Libertarianism isn't the progressive mission of constant reformation to rearrange power nor is it conservatism's push to preserve traditional institutional power. Libertarianism wants to enable every individual to determine their own power through voluntary means."

"When centralized institutions overstep like government, central banks and many social networks recently have I focus less on condemnation but exaltation of decentralized solutions in this case social networks like Mastodon and private money like crypto."

"Changing the political conversation is a balancing act between expressing an understanding and empathy with the average sensibilities and struggles of people while also breaking convention enough to open up the conversation to voices often not represented."

"A reminder that the constitution was meant to define the maximum role for government not the minimum. Just because it's authorized by the constitution doesn't mean it SHOULD be handled by government."

"Governments encourage you to do things by punishing you for not doing them. Markets encourage you by rewarding you (think insurance discounts for taking preventative actions). The former just doubles down if it doesn't work the latter innovates. I know which I prefer."

"A good leader listens because they know it will help them be heard. They work the front lines because it will inspire others to join them. A good leader isn't a leader at all, but a team member that keeps the team together, motivated and focused."

"We must live the Libertarian message to get others to embrace it. We must work to solve society's greatest challenges through our communities, charities and enterprises today and live the best case against government involvement."

"Should interest rates be high or low? Neither, they should be determined by the market where the interplay of loanable funds, the demand for them and risk help set rates and coordinate resources over time. I support monetary liberty unequivocally."□□

"Liberty ideals are grounded in reciprocity. I don't want to be stolen from, so I won't steal from you. I don't want to be hurt, so I won't hurt you. I want to live my values, so I'll let you live yours. The most powerful ideas are often the simplest ones."

"I love you and want to empower you regardless of your gender, gender identity, sexuality, religion, class, or even if you're not a fan of Doctor Who. Not all libertarians are as loving as me and that's ok as long as we don't hurt each other or take each other's stuff. I will work to preach love and hopefully people will choose to follow my lead."

"Your choice what you are known for.... Will it be making people aware of great ideas, great people and great actions or always being a curmudgeon about ideas, people and actions you don't love."

"What I love about Libertarianism is that it focuses on the journey more than the destination. Despite what others say, how you get somewhere does matter."

"To have a world where minimum force and maximum voluntarism can thrive, we need to be able to easily resolve our claims on scarce resources. Without property rights we'd live in a world of might makes right, not a world I desire."

"I avoid using the terms public and private because in people's minds you're saying "make available" vs "make unavailable" which is not what we're saying at all. We want to make a distinction between government property (whose funding, participation and use may be involuntary) vs Voluntary Property (where all funding, exchanges, and participation is voluntary and based on consent).

This is why I use the term Voluntarize instead of

privatize because it more accurately conveys my concerns and hopes as a libertarian."

"The left and right political establishments always want to pigeonhole #Libertarianism as an oppositional force. Libertarians are not conservative or progressive but individuals looking to bring back real governance and societal progress by promoting self-ownership.

The problem is when self-ownership is embraced it disempowers the corrupt structure of force that has played on your fears, hopes and frustrations to exercise power over you and strangle the economy to the point that we all struggle and blame each other for that struggle.

Libertarianism is about boundaries on power over others, it's about returning to you the power that has been taken over generations by alarmist politicians and special interests who have pitted us against each other.

Libertarianism isn't your enemy, it's theirs."

There is no perfect state of things. Although, we all have the natural tendency to adapt to changing circumstances. It's when adaptation is prevented everything begins to fall apart. Free people adapt.

Alex Merced
Vice Chair of the Libertarian National Committee

What matters to me is the ability for an individual to exercise their right to life, liberty and property. That is the focus, that is the goal. The structure, size and functioning of other institutions only matter to me relative to that core focus.

Alex Merced
Vice Chair of the Libertarian National Committee

AlexMerced.com - Libertarian101.com

87

Libertarians advocate for not getting into other people's business in our own lives, in domestic policy and in foreign policy. Minding your own business doesn't mean letting people push you around. People seem to get this confused when having historical discussions regarding foreign policy. The choice isn't only kill or be killed, coexistence is an option.

Alex Merced
Vice Chair of the Libertarian National Committee

If you want to help people, I encourage you to but I will not support forcing others to do so. If you need help, it's ok, we all have bad days and I encourage you to ask for help but don't ask me to force others to provide it. We all struggle, choose to help.

Alex Merced
Vice Chair of the Libertarian National Committee

AlexMerced.com - Libertarian101.com

Forcing people through government just tells me you are too impatient and lazy to learn how to inspire others to do great things and work together voluntarily.

Alex Merced
Vice Chair of the Libertarian National Committee

AlexMerced.com - Libertarian101.com

When any particular elected position, office or collection of offices have too much power polarization will grow. Why? It breeds a winner take all culture where one does not need to compromise or exercise empathy, just win and impose their will.

Alex Merced
Vice Chair of the Libertarian National Committee

Government, punishing poor people with taxation and regulations to fund appearing like they are helping the poor while enriching themselves and friends since forever.

Alex Merced
Vice Chair of the Libertarian National Committee

Regulations and Taxes are costs that get passed on to you via rising prices, lower quality, less jobs and lower investment returns. These effects will always have the most impact on those who have the least who'll become angry, seek a scapegoat and create polarization.

Alex Merced
Vice Chair of the Libertarian National Committee

AlexMerced.com - Libertarian101.com

War starts and continues when we look at each other as belonging to abstract collectives trying to displace the other. Peace occurs when we see each other's individual dreams, motivations and determination to thrive.

Alex Merced
Vice Chair of the Libertarian National Committee

AlexMerced.com - Libertarian101.com

We spend too much time trying to criticize each other by prodding at the limits of each other's beliefs instead of harvesting the treasure and beauty of the vast lands within them.

Alex Merced
Vice Chair of the Libertarian
National Committee

AlexMerced.com - Libertarian101.com

Free people don't lack problems and challenges, they just have the freedom to solve them.

Alex Merced
Vice Chair of the Libertarian National Committee

As a libertarian I'm fighting to allow individuals to be free to pursue their dreams, hopes and motivations in the If, how, who, what, where, when and why they associate with each other and exchange their justly acquired property.

Alex Merced
Vice Chair of the Libertarian National Committee

AlexMerced.com - Libertarian101.com

97

We often discuss "The Libertarian Mind", the ability to see opportunity cost in human choice, someone who can see the cost in knowledge and wealth when you limit choice and maximize coercion.

It's time to discuss "The Libertarian Heart", the compassion and empathy for those who are struggling in financial and personal fulfillment. The appreciation of how one can be empowered when you enable their ability to act towards fulfillment without the costs of artificial barriers and controls.

Alex Merced
Vice Chair of the Libertarian National Committee

AlexMerced.com - Libertarian101.com

Foreign Intervention often times audaciously tries to impose the interests and ideals of outsiders ignoring the motivations, divisions and economics of other nations often creating more instability not less. Non-Intervention is about humility and respect for the world.

Alex Merced
Vice Chair of the Libertarian National Committee

AlexMerced.com - Libertarian101.com

The more centralized
and monopolistic
decision making becomes
not only the less informed
it will be but the less
consideration of humanity
it will contain.

Alex Merced
Vice Chair of the Libertarian
National Committee

Artificial costs (Taxes, Tariffs, Regulations, Inflation) Create real struggle. Real struggle creates resentment, hostility and division as people scapegoat those who "appear" to get relief at their expense. Reduce costs, reduce struggle, reduce division.

Alex Merced
Vice Chair of the Libertarian National Committee

AlexMerced.com - Libertarian101.com

Prohibition creates crime and enhances harm of what it prohibits while pushing any social challenges into the shadow where it can't be measured or dealt with. Add in the economic/social effects of mass incarceration you got to ask yourself, why?

Alex Merced
Vice Chair of the Libertarian National Committee

AlexMerced.com - Libertarian101.com

Libertarianism is appealing to everyone, because at the end of the day libertarianism is really just an appeal to who you want to be, and everyone can appeal to their own sense of self. The question always is people's fear of each other. People have no problem with the freedom to be themselves. They're scared of what happens when other people are themselves, and how that will effect them. That's why the libertarian message is one of hope and tolerance, because in order to have a world where we can let each other be free, we can't be scared of each other. That's a very different conversation than the other parties are having, which is why the Libertarian Party is a unique vehicle, the only vehicle that can change the conversation, reduce fear and polarization, and create a world where we can just let each other be.

Alex Merced
Vice Chair of the Libertarian National Committee

AlexMerced.com - Libertarian101.com

The way your ideas are framed and presented have implications that go beyond policy. It also frames how people think about the challenges around them and whether they have any ability to surmount them. Give people truth but also hope.

Alex Merced
Vice Chair of the Libertarian National Committee

AlexMerced.com - Libertarian101.com

LEARN MORE

Libertarian101.com
AlexMerced.com
LearnEconomicsNow.com
BitcoinBlockchainCrypto.com
IntroToLiberty.com

JOIN MY MAILING LIST

TheList.AlexMerced.com

BUY SOME T-SHIRTS

Tshirts.AlexMerced.Com